British Standards

Also by Robert Sheppard (* *published by Shearsman Books*)

Poetry
The Flashlight Sonata
Transit Depots/Empty Diaries (with John Seed [text] and Patricia Farrell [images])
Empty Diaries
The Lores
Tin Pan Arcadia
Hymns to the God in which My Typewriter Believes
Complete Twentieth Century Blues
Warrant Error *
Berlin Bursts *
The Given
A Translated Man *
Words Out of Time
Unfinish
History or Sleep — Selected Poems *
Twitters for a Lark (co-authored) *
Micro Event Space
Bad Idea
The English Strain *

Fiction
The Only Life

Edited
Floating Capital: New Poets from London (with Adrian Clarke)
News for the Ear: A Homage to Roy Fisher (with Peter Robinson)
The Salt Companion to Lee Harwood
The Door at Taldir: Selected Poems of Paul Evans *
Atlantic Drift: an anthology of poetry and poetics (with James Byrne)
New Collected Poems of Lee Harwood (with Kelvin Corcoran) *
Mary Robinson: *Selected Poems* *

Criticism
Far Language: Poetics and Linguistically Innovative Poetry 1978–1997
The Poetry of Saying: British Poetry and Its Discontents 1950–2000
Iain Sinclair
When Bad Times Made for Good Poetry *
The Meaning of Form in Contemporary Innovative Poetry
The Necessity of Poetics *

On Robert Sheppard
The Robert Sheppard Companion, ed. Byrne & Madden *

Robert Sheppard

British Standards

The English Strain, Book Three

Shearsman Books

First published in the United Kingdom in 2024 by
Shearsman Books
PO Box 4239
Swindon
SN3 9FN

Shearsman Books Ltd Registered Office
30–31 St. James Place, Mangotsfield, Bristol BS16 9JB
(this address not for correspondence)

www.shearsman.com

ISBN 978-1-84861-935-7

Copyright © Robert Sheppard, 2024

The right of Robert Sheppard to be identified as the author
of this work has been asserted by him in accordance with the
Copyrights, Designs and Patents Act of 1988.
All rights reserved.

CONTENTS

Preface: England in 2019	7
Poems of National Independence: liberties with Wordsworth	8
Double Standards 1: Political Greatness	23
14 Standards	24
Double Standards 2: Big Data and Little Bo	39
Tabitha and Thunderer: Interventions in Mary Robinson's *Sappho and Phaon*	40
Ozymandias: a dub of Shelley	48
Weird Syrup	49
1: Contrafacts and Counterfactuals from Keats	50
2: Curtal Song-Nets from Junkets	64
Lift not the Painted Veil: an overdub of Shelley	74
Unth(reading) Clare	75
Astral Zen Knickers: overdub of Shelley's 'To Wordsworth'	97
Partly from Hartley: two double sonnets	99
To Laughter: an overdub of Shelley	101
After Laughter	102
Notes and Acknowledgements	110

Have you read Wordsworth's anti-railroad Sonnets? As Petrarch with all his Sonnets could never prevail on Laura to more than admire him, ... how could the Bard imagine or fancy that 14 lines, though each line were instinct with living fire like an Electric Telegraph, would mollify the philanthropic no-heart of a Railway Company?
—Hartley Coleridge 1847

Preface

England in 2019
an overdub of Shelley

A middle-aged groper without majority
his cabinet sealed in the dark like rats
through public scorn of *all* politicians
governs with blind faith without facts
They won the 'war' without firing a shot – except
at Jo Cox in whose memory he 'gets Brexit done'! –
He'll do what he does best which is nothing
stage his coup at near Peter's Field rant riots and prisons
Global ecocide is beside his point his
hedge fund backers bet on no-deal
In blackout Parliament Time runs down statutes
He'll repeal and revoke and pull the people's plug –
But perhaps Caretaker Corbyn will rattle his keys
use his flashlight to locate the burst fusebox in time

3rd October 2019

Poems of National Independence

liberties with Wordsworth

In honoured poverty thy voice did weave
Songs consecrate to truth and liberty, –
Deserting these, thou leavest me to grieve,
Thus having been, that thou shouldst cease to be.

Shelley, 'To Wordsworth'

*JONES! as from Calais southward you and I
Went pacing side by side, this public Way
Streamed with the pomp of a too-credulous day,
When faith was pledged to new-born Liberty:
A homeless sound of joy was in the sky:
From hour to hour the antiquated Earth
Beat like the heart of Man: songs, garlands, mirth,
Banners, and happy faces, far and nigh!
And now, sole register that these things were,
Two solitary greetings have I heard,
'Good-morrow, Citizen!' a hollow word,
As if a dead man spake it! Yet despair
Touches me not, though pensive as a bird
Whose vernal coverts winter hath laid bare.*

William Wordsworth 7th August 1802

Fair Star of evening, Splendour of the west

Big Bong at eleven, resonant in the North, voice
of *my* country, strong across swart horizon, above
White Cliff's Union Jack screen, carries like Big Bo
stooping over Britannia's spangled party bosom,
on the government's news feed; Bo's little bong
on the Number Ten gong (the Cum's boohooing!)
conspicuous to all nations – but not on the BBC.
This bong is my country's new anthem! Winking,
laughing, Bo waves his bombastic banners over
his fresh duties, puzzled, declares, *There, this
dark spot is Global Britain's sphere.* Sport thrives
under Go's new National Thrust. Bought spent men
linger with contempt, do not love *her*, my fingered
Kentish maiden flattened against freezing winter metal.

6th February 2020

Is it a reed that's shaken by the wind

Regard the dogging camps flooded by Storm Bo,
my lords, liars, statesmen. We use face
recognition to *detect* the viral sick, *detain*
the feral poor, *deport* the febrile black! Bend
the law; lengthen sentences: legislate in haste!
These are the first fruits of office, unseemly
reverence to Bo's shuffling power. Brush
off the squirts with low yielding arts degrees.
Level up the local level crossings. Plough HS2
through the nookie-moist nooks of English ground.
Build bridges between our crumbling colonies. Tilt
the level playing field of Euro-trade in gems.
'Shame on you!' they cry as Priti leaves the
chamber, shaken by her stormy rush of wind.

13th February 2020

Jones! As from Calais southward you and I

Trev! We streamed south to Charlton Athletic
to see Pete Townshend skid across the stage.
We chanted, 'Won't Get Fooled Again.' We were,
despite the pledge to 'not reason and compare'.
On campus, *Socialist Worker* was hawked
by a walk-on from Talcy-Malcy's *History Man*.
There were songs and banners and dopy smiles:
the roach end of that revolution had cooled.
'Morning, comrade!' a live man at the rally cries;
my genial spirits lift as we drift to St. George's Hall.
Our well-heeled heels trip over the homeless,
sleeping like birds under Amazon cardboard.
Now, focused on zero hours and pensions,
the only word that registers is *No!*

17th February 2020

Festivals have I seen that were not names

It's Bonaparty Bo's birthday party –
every day! Swaying on Carrie's motorbike,
he's petrolled his way into the history books
already, in the English in which *Gastarbeiters*
must henceforth beg for their revocable visas,
chanting a Brexit Festival chorus of National
Facts. Calais's not happy. Along the sea-coast,
migrants escaped *from* Britain, denounce our
charter deportations (in perfect English). Where
once Wyatt and Surrey, Wellington and Churchill,
waged eloquent war, we will again bulk-buy fags,
vomiting *vino* on our shoes. Safe on our shores
we shall sing: *We don't need no human rights
doing our business in our own backyard*

20th February 2020

Toussaint, the most unhappy man of men!

Flat-Battery Bo, rusticated man's man!
Can you hear the lactating maids moaning
in the liberal groves of Chevening, while
you lie heeding no more than the two A4 sheet
briefings allotted by the Cum? Oh, miserable chief –
no time to scan them? Are you dead drunk,
or are you cackling in madman's chains, Sabisky's
eugenics? Your powers can't work against air,
earth and sky. Coronavirus breathes on the very wind
that brings the floods, yet you don't appear in mask,
with mop. You have great allies: Useless Eustace
exults lactic chicky washes, Bully Beef Patel delivers
agonies to her staff; but only you have rich
unconquerable love for your impenetrable mind.

24th February 2020

We had a female Passenger who came from Calais

In your fidgety revisions, she's 'a fellow-passenger…
from Calais' (tracking today's trafficking route);
'gaudy in array' you wrote, though 'spotless' is
nobler, this 'Negro woman' now 'white-robed'
in your neo-Netflix pot of time. 'Downcast' was
suggestive, 'silent' merely sufficient. Coleridgean
'dejected' becomes De Quinceyean 'destitute' (as
the female vagrants of *our* Age of Immiseration).
You confess to speaking to the 'expelled' (we use
the term 'deported'); 'kindness' chills to 'intercourse'.
Her eyes 'burning independent' frame her alone, yet
'driv'n from France' called out the Hostile Environment.
But did you wonder *who* she was, this Toussaint sister?
You fail to revise the racist rhyme of 'face'.

27th February/2nd March 2020

Here, on our native soil, we breathe once more

Here, with naked breasts, they soil once more.
The cocks that crowd round the cooling motors,
the blasts of horn; – those boys and rarer girls
in white t-shirts, loosened boxers, hoisted skirts,
playing with themselves (and each other) – all,
all are English. I've often stalked with joy in
Kent's dogging fields, but never satisfied myself
so much as seeing and hearing these warming hands
octopussying through car windows over ripened ripples.
Europe is in bondage: fuck 'em! You're free,
my country. My Companion sucks this bloke.
I sense his perfect bliss, his veiny tool scented
like a gynaecologist's probe. She spits his
libation onto the trodden grass of England.

1st March 2020

Inland, within a hollow vale, I stood

In England, within Kent's greenest vale, I stooped
among nettles, heard waves breaking, air thick
with fearful virus coughed over the coast of France,
the border of old Europe. I shrank, a hollow tube
after last night's fervent intercourse, skirting
The Daily Mail's 'most frightful neighbourhood'.
Migrants flood from dinghies, spot doggers' delight:
a mighty good show of wicked wives, spouting geezers,
blowing and rolling in Britain's new-found liberty.
God help them! They're nothing in themselves,
these literal super-spreaders literally gone viral. When
emergency decrees bark at *them*, banning faceless men
in chunky jumpers, erotic seafood unfolding
for their tide, only the Nation's grandees shall be free.

5th March 2020

O Friend! I know not which way I must look

Parts of Bo want to look away (it wasn't meant
to be like this!) comfort in the great oppression.
Dressing in a mask is just for show,
like Naomi Campbell's empty airport hazmat chic!
The wealthiest among us are best protected.
The handyman and the cook have been laid off
below the sick pay threshold, to build up 'herd
immunity' in the herd, wheezing at sports events,
coughing in open libraries over closed books. Plain
thinking gives way to the Cum's behavioural data,
predicting our supposed crisis fatigue, acceptable loss.
Bo prays we must 'take it on the chin' for the economy,
chants 'Buller! Buller! Buller!' as he rinses his trotters,
huffs back to his breathing, breeding, household.

13th March 2020

Milton! thou shouldst be living at this hour

Cummings, Britain hath no need of thee! You've
found your swamp to drain. Religiomaniacs,
fruit salad generals, poets laureate (no friends,
but I defend, like Milton), even your puppet's
National Thrust, where, naked under heavens,
majestic sticks, in Lethean flood, stick – *all* are forfeit
to your 'scientific' elite: 'complex contagions in a
thermoacoustic system' modelling our insecurity
from starter home to care home, neatly monetized.
The intelligent rich (a moron's oxymoron) claim
only selfish men may raise us up, return to power. Free
Dom, self-isolation is your viral wet dream, of use,
your voice white noise in a Seeing Room's drone.
Bo's cheerful hand rests on your thoroughbred's thigh.

16th March 2020

Great men have been among us; hands that penned

Now Viral Men have been among us, hands
unwashed, tongues speckled with disease,
I yearn for touchy-feely Drayton, Browning, Smith,
vain Surrey, wicked Wyatt, minatory Milton,
and the moral of their sonnets of selfhood,
environment and socius, transposed (by me!),
before this Age of Self-Isolation and social
distance, Bo's 'inalienable free-born right to go
to the pub', reluctantly, frozen. France,
trussed in transnational infection-data exchange,
perpetual empty boulevards in lockdown, is all virus
and no genius. As Bo says: '*We* live in a land
of liberty, but we rule nothing out.' Nothing
fills his want of the skilled low paid like nothing.

21st March 2020

One might believe that natural miseries

One might well believe that national misery
only blasted Britain, made it a void land
unfit for labour: rural workers dwell on
sofas, ordinary businessmen tap online.
Bright sun and breeze herd them to the weekend parks,
for their sensual pleasures, soothing flesh, no cares.
Myriads must work – against themselves. 'No more
Brexit frenzy, no more drunken mirth!' cries Bo.
The Great Libertarian has switched off the
lights!… This sonnet has been interrupted to
deliver the latest lockdown laughter to
your doorstep. Watch this spot while the Cum spumes: 'Herd
immunity, protect the economy,
and if that means some pensioners die, too bad.'

25th March 2020

England! The time is come when thou shouldst wean

Britain, the time is now to wean yourself from
hoarding fancy food or panic buying bog rolls.
It's hard. Old routines are unsettled. Seedy spots
where you trespassed (camera phones in one hand),
idly watched at bridlepaths for meat-wagons
freighting broad-shouldered flesh, are shut, policed
by drones. If in Italy, Spain, France, Germany,
they falter, how will proud Brexit Britain fare?
It lost the email inviting it to share with them.
We self-isolating 'get well' card rhymesters
(the abject position of the contemporary poet now,
according to the press, and even some bards;
we must soothe and smooth the national mood) gift
Bo our best wishes: *Our prime hopes rest with you!*

28th March 2020

Vanguard of Liberty, ye men of Kent

Vanloads of libertines, playboys of Kent,
you once set your calcic frowns against
France's toothless coast! Now's the time
to prove you're rock hard tarts! Let Gillray's
Bum-Boats dump the last of your hops. Those
French hear your brave woodland shouts for show
as you roam, single, in self-distancing self-love;
they watch your glistening lance throb
in your (well-washed) hand, as you film
an isolated maiden in a mask. 'She's a *nurse!*'
No partying now: we're ramping up mass testing,
damping down individual urges. In breathless
Bo's Britain, each stay-indoors chartered street
is mothballed in his notional socialism.

31st March 2020

Double Standards 1

Political Greatness
an overdub of Shelley

Bo's Brexit joy, Bo's majority, Bo's fame –
Bo's lifted from muddle by the skill of the Cum.
They shepherd the masked herd beyond immunity.

They sing revisionary ballads, history scrubbed free
of pre-lockdown shame and *Stay Alert* shambles.
While millions mourned in self-enforced oblivion,

treading customary pageant round the park,
dumb Cum drove virus to the pre-hotspot North,
tested his sick eyes: *That's Barney Castle…*

Obscene display enough, retrospective small print
exceptionalism. Quell anarchy's juggled hope and fear.
The slob scrubbed up well to recant – then didn't.

Either you follow blind instinct or the one rule that
remains: humans must rule the dominion of themselves.

25th May 2020

14 Standards

It was a night of storms in the world above us; and, far below the surface of the earth as we were, the murmur of the winds, sighing through the passages, came on my ear like the voices of the departed, – like the pleadings of the dead. Involuntarily I fixed my eye on the manuscript I was to copy, and never withdrew till I had finished its extraordinary contents.
  —Charles Robert Maturin, *Melmoth the Wanderer*

Poem Against the Slave Trade III

Oh he is worn with toil! the big drops run
Down his dark cheek; hold – hold thy merciless hand,
Pale tyrant! for beneath thy hard command
O'erwearied Nature sinks. The scorching Sun,
As pityless as proud Prosperity,
Darts on him his full beams; gasping he lies
Arraigning with his looks the patient skies,
While that inhuman trader lifts on high
The mangling scourge. Oh ye who at your ease
Sip the blood-sweeten'd beverage! thoughts like these
Haply ye scorn: I thank thee Gracious God!
That I do feel upon my cheek the glow
Of indignation, when beneath the rod
A sable brother writhes in silent woe.

Robert Southey

1

To the River

Boss Bo's wandering hand stirs the spirit
of those stuck in the world with a single pose
watching crumbling profit margins disappear
in a mighty wave plug the ear of pity

for Bo's faith in the arrival of pre-lockdown
trains under Arriva franchise touches us all
blue ribbon Mersey free fringed with mist
my Muse eyes the bank lone impassive

returning theatre diverts his wandering wave
the soothing calm of presidential disinfectant
thrills in Bo's nightmare throat he spills

his cleanest *mots* under his trembling mighty
hand as I sing he speaks of passing peaks of
grit and guts his wonted pride *thumbs-up emojis*

2

To a Friend, Who Asked How I Felt,
When the Nurse First Presented My Infant to Me
by Samuel Taylor Coleridge

At dawn's first coffee   I scan my passport
to prove my self   through a sycamore
sun bursts   into the leaf-time of breathless spring
update your face in the mirror   it has angel's form

It's left without you   appears in this poem
a sudden father   dewy on his mobile
in a public callbox   for old time's sake
imagine giving   birth in a pandemic

Priti disappointed   Bo's thrilled and melted
that any thing   could be 'powered by love'
she puckers the frigid   kiss of the State
for the   fever lips of the 'economic inactive'

Watch the parasite   feed off beauty
who still thinks PPE is what rich kids   *do* at Oxford

3

The Vanity of National Grandeur

It took Covid-19 to topple Bo's giddy lust,
zigzagging virality of virility. The bong-gong
his near knell. He shifted Victory (over) Europe Day
around his post-Brexit holiday calendar. Adjust

in Time. The cheated hand waves the pennant to
We're Meat Again as spitfires spit universal spores.
Labour is a sponge squeezed dry. Who was that Masked
Psilosopher? My curious hand shakes at his suffictions.

A consolation consul, he's got a creamy tub of poesy
into which he stirs radicalism like jam. *Frontline*
is always somewhere/somebody else, hi-viz patrols
to broken train tracks. Thunder affords unsympathetic
background, scowling backdrop to his latest Skype.
His pocket awakes into rising alarm.

4

Poem on the Slave Trade
                    by Robert Southey

weary to tears of staying home
the heroism of inaction
twist your ankle on Tarleton
empty of trade your cry silent
the monitor on mute
as clear as pro-saccharrites
now only the freeborn low-skilled
may wrap themselves in bin bags
to entertain big drops of viral sweat
dumping cubes and neuroleptic blocks
pale sun sweeps the sleepers off Bold St
the furloughed barista or barrister asks (at

last) how many slave owners does
it take to sweeten a cup of coffee

5

To a Young Lady, Purposing to Marry a Man of Immoral Character in the Hope of his Reformation

Time we cannot take away
                         from him forgives him
Every time forfeits a blonde
                         or two to his fancy this
Lawless libertine rooting for vice
                         leading you astray
With promises and cut-price
                         pre-nups supping your
Juices with *Tignanello*
                         Bountiful Bo mortific before
Nascent data shoving the herd with
                         energic Cum He
Resurrects at Easter
                         and unto to you a boy is born

6

The Idiot Girl
by Mary F. Johnson

Her level of fantasy was alarming.
Her tone dirge-like, she'd received tokens of love in a stupefying trance.
Some of her audience was crying with laughter.
She tossed her long red hair 'creatively'.
A deluded child with a doting mother fostering her cloistered intensity,
    shielded from scrutiny or routine.
Ideas inbred, she scribbled non-stop in her notebooks: Pre-Raphaelite
    doodles, biomorphic ornaments, groping fallopians.
Flicked a fully inked page over, to begin again under down-curling hair,
    her mother on the ground, her grandmother in the attic
    bedroom with 'sunset windfarms in the bay'.
An ode to her porch, loose stones, insular solitude.
She palmed away advice as our replacement bus squeezed round a
    country town corner to pass *Luigi's Flying Scissors*.
The train came to rest at Liverpool – people scrabbled out of its stifling
    lack of air con.
Record how un-endearing she was, ungenerous but true.
A month into lockdown, silent streets fill with glad clappers for key
    workers.
I spot a newsclip of her wailing on the steps of the Crown Court: an
    etiolated corpse found locked in her windowless loft.
She blocked the porch with her final words: 'My grandmother's self-
    isolating, and will not come down!'

7

Weed drips into water   silent
As lockdown streets   low cloud rolls
Over unrolling news   emotive tide
That may not be stemmed   'operation
Last gasp' co-opted to Bo's canonised
Breath   police stop the jogging mother
With her skipping daughter   blot clouds
Billow inked lake   super moon   thin cover
Ministers cramping up testimonials
Before futurity's magpies   bleached streak of
Ruffled hair wrinkles across the wildlife
Soundtrack   the park growls   authority's
Inexorable frown   binding before our eyes
Each roomy sonnet locked with a hermit's clue

8

        now windows open on a
different world
        hushed streets empty
of thronging bands breeze
        stale the trickle of breached pipes
under paving between drains
        routine buckles these oars of fire
dipped into treacle lake
        under flaming sirens
ambulances whine as anxiety pools
        red wine below floorboards keeps
time to stern brooding
        fruity with breath's
imagined judgement

9

Ozymandias
by Horace Smith

crown strips
historic pitch flaking virus on hot plastic
car seats parked at testing centres you've
no thing to express police crunching shells
pour cold water on distancing day's blue
wash fist threatens mist wiped Brighton's stony
silence dispersed in spores you leap under
the pier for long nights gulls pound
pared dash of rubble sound harbours the
annihilated everyday looks to you as principle
of looking for mountain goats come down
from their nominal mountains wolves in cheesecloth
buried ear worm undegradable latex glove long
washed free of its grubby fetish waves
from its pebbly pork chop barbie cromlech

10

Written in the Workhouse

I'm 'addicted to furlough', binge-reading, Time
on my washed-raw hands. If this is lockdown, Big
Bo's the governor. He confesses he's a
porker like us inmates: we go to the morgue
quicker than svelte Svens. I gorge on prose to breathe
out poetry, locked in with Maturin, lost
on the sickbed with Perdita. I snack on
Minton's Westbrook *Blake*, Byron's Woolwich Free, bob
in Raghavan's propulsive wash, wave off his
calls to action. Standards: *Solitude* springs fresh,
recorded by Kandace, *Recorda Me* on
Braxton's pip-squeak sopranino. No time to
think about reviewing the book of reviews
that reviews the books I've already reviewed.

11

When lovers' lips from kissing disunite
by Charles Tennyson Turner

Move back from her breaking lips. Taste
as soft as melting fruit. They'd have to tunnel
through time to reach the free world now. Her
first words ushered to the night are fraught
with breathless thoughts of 'wealth *or* health'

Revelation unburdens in the boudoir.
Suspended rights. One regulation afternoon
spent dodging a jogger whose merest huff's
deadly as gunshot. Zigzag tacks across the grass

The nearest kiss is a memory-print on electric
skin. Thrills still pledge where thrusts are deep
and long. Slip from history's distant night

Doves fight over an olive branch. Crows
scrabble for negative crumbs on silent slates

12

Long time a child, and still a child
by Hartley Coleridge

you were that child
        and still your fight's there in the
                distanced classroom
blond man-boys rattle their toys
                      in their own echoes
your father strode the station foyer
                attracting government spies
     his thought-pulses becoming song

shelter inside this sonnet to exchange
            the stock history of the avant-garde
for loose strands from the sociopath's weave

     we won a race that never ran
squatting in squat watchtowers to watch
             failure in December blight us in May

13

The Dancing Girl
by Letitia Elizabeth Landon

  this is the darkest time though colour fields   I
   flex and shimmer in the retinal pool eyes   don't
    shoot dance through thin surfaces this is   want
     a weary world flattened indoors into   to
      fresh-faced images of fresher faces seen   just
       (as they seem) less clearly for our lesser   make
        looking she takes the breath she slices moulds form
       its feeling vibrations in creaking knees she   the
       lifts the line of poetry to shift the limbs   plastic
      we open the shutters to let in light   hope
     to sharpen all the hopes to harp-notes   of
    and unshackle the air and shape the ear she   hope
   stretches in crooked space to bend it   itself

14

A Dance of Nymphs
by Dante Gabriel Rossetti

music passively carried to trace thought to the sense

      nymphs' feet think his bitter tears kick
      the rock proving his limbs melting into water
      suggest government scientists' passive brains
      need the active interruption of diaphanous drapes
      take us all back to when one whiff of sweat
      meant the world white peaches float where
      he leans across bent thought most human as
      she's cock-slapped by a randy god leaping
      from behind his predictive dynamics into
      the tear-stained abandon of his human fears
      a pang of throbbing meat senses the sense
      the work starts counting from one not zero

meaning I believe felt each blind portion of pulse

April–May 2020

Double Standards 2

Big Data and Little Bo

> *an overdub of Shelley's*
> 'Feelings of a Republican on the Fall of Bonaparte'

Feelings!? I loathe, and oppose, you,
unfallen tyro of Brexit Year Zero. Ambitious
unelect-élite, after your mythic drive, you reverse

hard over the (metaphorical) bodies you hid. Bo
fears your blog or biog, blocks your dismissal.
You flip up a laptop to monitor his ministers. Go

moans: *I customarily drive miles to test my eyesight!* Bo
defrauds and deforces the law so that you had not broken it,
a legal crime. Your blogpost namedrops the virus in

retrospective egghead prescience. Allow *me* to un-write
history, re-form Shelley: you slouch toward the Rose Garden
in this re-drafted poem, revised statement in hand…

Too late! You and Bo are in the murky clear.
It's a high-skill job to unblock Bo's foulest passage.

28th May 2020

Tabitha and Thunderer

Sappho and Phaon XIII:
She Endeavours to Fascinate Him

Bring, bring to deck my brow, ye Sylvan girls,
A roseate wreath; nor for my waving hair
The costly band of studded gems prepare,
Of sparkling crysolite or orient pearls:
Love, o'er my head his canopy unfurls,
His purple pinions fan the whisp'ring air;
Mocking the golden sandal, rich and rare,
Beneath my feet the fragrant woodbine curls.
Bring the thin robe, to fold about my breast,
White as the downy swan; while round my waist
Let leaves of glossy myrtle bind the vest,
Not idly gay, but elegantly chaste!
Love scorns the nymph in wanton trappings drest;
And charms the most concealed, are doubly grac'd.

Mary Robinson

Tabitha and Thunderer:
Interventions in Mary Robinson's Sappho and Phaon

> *There is a dead female poet*
> *in my pants*
>   —Prudence Bussey-Chamberlain

Why when my stare turns Thunderer
into sugar does he melt desire back
into himself why his shadow stains
the warshipped streets blood flowing over
the hot pillow of my tongue Teams
on mute the liar tosses his head was
I just a melting lay a body abused
songbird strung with passion shoes off
downtime gin special advisors tip
soft vibrations smooth my silent lips with
hum and moan unmute he speechifies
another mock enquiry on the *matter* of
barbary (I keep slipping centuries triumphal
statues slide headstrong into my wet dock

Why not in aching caresses I used to start
while my tangle of curls entangled him
in tangles of desire for these very curls
bare back shameful blush in vain pushes
through veins veiled in my vale no more
a lyric professor of subjectivity I
narrate my self bathed in sprinkled
scorched source of song-thrill
Go my Mamas with no papas shiver
your shoulders why must Thunderer's stunted
slaves slice through viral Liverpool streets vile
African Trade banners swaying while I
miraculate angles my heels force on him he'll
melt like Bo kicking fit on his office floor

You who from dark alleys across
pleasure gardens romping rude-
girls to Bo's 'fantastic' taproom
you glide with nutrients flaunt
fallen tresses from fresh hairdos
you worship her Lord of Lust
his Tarleton crop as he thumps
out thunder like Boozy Bo bashes
the podium-truth he re-opens his
war wounds his meat cleaver
moment shares his Instagram war
crimes and they shower his vagabond
shoes how can she salve this slaver as
she tweaks her strings her throbbing muff

Bring feathery fascinator from
furloughed Ascot tickle a studied
look in domino mask my trim
weather girls sweep your slender arms
across the cyclone of my breast circle
the purple advance of his tropical
thunder Woodbines outside the bookie he
checks his phone bring me cheap bling
my thin red bra-straps tingle his fingers
pull corset stays tight make him stay
push me into new shapes shoot him
off spill him limp into my braided wheat-
ear lap so I may shut the book of
his arousal and begin to narrate my own

Now my sunflower greets my girls
like Rishi beaming with vouchers
droop your heads over Thunderer's
thighs aroused by cash-bells my un-
furloughed shop-girls spill laxative seed

upon his sweaty vest sink him in my fragrant
hollow (nostrils flaring) to taste me finger me
with phantom tips in his haunting breakfast
glow now tease him out of lockdown track
him trace him test him for a fortnight
necking nectar flatter his flattened heart
blind him with steaming towels now
open him up like a Turkish barbershop
flash his steel and steal his thunder

Why plunderer love is a virus flips
mouth to mouth Perdita's lost the
lottery again promised to the shady bank
that milks you through silk breeches
half a plantation in one Faro afternoon
I keep my royal jewels in place
hold abandonment in check as
you cover me vagrant on the fragrant bank
of your negative income-stream I promise to
bare one creamy breast you trace its generous
vein I'll slip out of pure lust's chemise chilled
by your levelling up burning for your
stamping down numb as you fail Bo's
'sure-bet nomination' to *his* privy council

Farewell dead-drops farewell my registry
girls cracking codes farewell
Russian babes longing in golden coves
swapping cases by royal benches at Kew
strings broken across leopard-skin thighs
uncrossed crossing Bo mesmerised by
oligarchs waving ash-tipped cigarettes
Thunderer sinks to the carpet liars spout
schoolboy Greek couched in conch he
licks his stubby fingers tongue fresh

from salty crevices of caviar-devils
pleasured with cocaine their cupped
palms pour his excess off while
Tabitha helps out by eating out

On Brighton beach he thunders
lightning darts around his darkening
eyes in the surge pleading I tear
my spume-drenched limbs
sea foams over my bleeding
breasts the tide-sucked pebbles
seethe withdrawal as he flees
to Parisian salad-pickers with
Marie Antoinette necklines
waiting in line for his flinty
pork chopper while Little Bo
Pop barks that *Covid fatties*
cost their own *bleak lives* the
only pounds worth losing

Tabitha is thin disguise for my she-voice!
She's not going to throw herself from
the Leucadian Rock for Thunderer, a rake
lifted from Gillray and dropped over
tight-trousered war-criminal slaver-gambler Tarleton,
because of his one 'low caprice'! Clockwork logic
ordains multiple faintings and frequent droppings-dead!
Perdita, re-thread the rhymes through this season's muslin.
I take back control of Sappho's voice
her lyre in my steady hand tremulous vibration
It holds my sovereign breath
a little trauma to trigger controlled delirium
I take back control of Sappho's form
the ninth gem in my corona turns its glitter silver

A chorus of gulls caws coronas of pain
above the cliffs towards Beachy Head
(that reads like one of chalky Charlie-Girl's
props!) Cheer up my cheerleading girls
I take back control of The *English* Sappho
Androgynous desire made him my neatest explosion
his receding hairline his testosteronic myth
breeding the virus along our 'haunted beach'
My frown's wedged over the slits of my eyes
The fateful vessel rocks at Brighton pier
Britain I quit your pebbly Brexscinded shore
sucking itself off like Matthew Arnold
I've taken back control of English poetry
My heroines transfigure into bigger

'Maid is he' may be just a typo (it's not)
but it transports *him* beyond timid curiosity
He's rubbing himself on fraying silk
with his beauteous arm in 'that gay bower'
an ebony cage rigged for saccharine slavery
bent over a Turkish pouféé in pleasure's torture
and there's really nothing poetry can do about it
I want to suck his face off like a cartoon
The sweetest bud pines open for the bee O
women let's take back control of poetic justice
Let's share his manhole like rats and superheroine
Our practised touch is enough to shrink his balls
It's not *whether* to wear the strap on
It's which shaft I'll select to shift his excessive joy

Abyssinian Maid follow me from this beach
to where clouds bled blue by thin sky puff your fame
He visualised a seaside dome of pleasure here
with egg nog ale and what the butler saw but
I *heard* your chants warbled like a Fado queen

Follow me out of lockdown and we'll play again
sweet echoes' passing resemblance to nothing
He damns poetic language for its lack of control
He bites my tongue I slip it bleeding deep in his mouth
to demusicate 'debate' about Brexsanguinated Britain
I take back control of poetic artifice
struggle with its corsetry to achieve strange beauty
Lend me your dulcimer and I'll pluck its metaphor
to compose one more sonnet about the sonnet that isn't

Come women from my nine-a-side
scrum down on the bed each crumple
crumples uniquely zig zag round
the aura of Erato her avatar bore this
for several nights as ceremony
we take back the Euro trophy a spray
of princely lilies as stalks flip leaves over
pitted visages the woman who isn't there
is a labour of light shaped like herself
throwing her shoulder for us to weep on
with slight shudders and stifled moans
the sprinkler on the showerhead droops
and drips pearls that patter the pat
apologies of his vanishing pity. Pity

Dizzy with passion not testing my eyes
eyeballing a smug eagle as it poses
lofty against a final sunset I muse why
would anyone mummify a crocodile
using leaves ripped from my *Beauties*
To be human is to be dishevelled
Down below I see a stream of living lust
spawned from Poseidon into the waves
he wanks white horses under Bo's White Cliffs
to put me off perishing from this precipice

He dives seals liars into pelagic lairs I must
take back love's dread control and plunge into
the pool that masks initial touching
and find the designated place to make love

20th June–8th August 2020

Ozymandias: *a dub of Shelley* [1]

2

                                                                                 3

               4 5

      6

                                           7

             8 9

---

[1] This statue has been removed for further study.[a]

[2] The level plinth.

[3] They didn't roll this hollow monster to the harbour in '81. He was dropped where he'd stood, eyeing the monarch's approach. Replaced by a single shivering palm, a Jamaican flag for *ganja* Bank Holidays.

[4] So stiff that one Mohican turf surrealises him, just beyond history, well beyond 'Mohican'.

[5] 'Barefoot in sand': Bare facts for the unknown, boundless space for the disappeared.

[6] Along the shore, the Iron Men socially distance.[b]

[7] Self-besotted be-sooted Bo; be-suited Go. In bronze!

[8] 'A vast Trump of Stone': The White House forced to discreet enquiry concerning vacancies at Mount Rushmore.

[9] Any toppled statue becomes a sculpture in shatters of re-form, memories of its memory.

     [a] See '*Ozymandias* by Horace Smith' in '14 Standards', and its note.
     [b] *Another Place*, Anthony Gormley, Crosby.

Weird Syrup

On First Looking into Chapman's Homer

Much have I travell'd in the realms of gold,
And many goodly states and kingdoms seen;
Round many western islands have I been
Which bards in fealty to Apollo hold.
Oft of one wide expanse had I been told
That deep-brow'd Homer ruled as his demesne;
Yet did I never breathe its pure serene
Till I heard Chapman speak out loud and bold:
Then felt I like some watcher of the skies
When a new planet swims into his ken;
Or like stout Cortez when with eagle eyes
He stared at the Pacific—and all his men
Look'd at each other with a wild surmise—
Silent, upon a peak in Darien.

John Keats

1. Contrafacts and Counterfactuals from Keats

On Looking Again into Peter Hughes's *Petrarch*

I've travelled a lot in North
Norfolk too I've seen toffs

with their hunting guns eating
their own packed lunches in

the pubs faced the snippy
crabs of crumbling Cromer

the nippy Arctic blizzards
of Blakeney Point I've seen

washed-out Teddy Boys
weeping in Norwich Market

yet never did I find
a tattered fairground

blaring *Stupid Cupid* through
a distorted tannoy till

I heard sly Peter
loud and clear and felt

like a post-Brexit Europhile
gifted my first starry visa

or like I'd watched Eric
Morecambe on telly

with his trembling glasses
stretching over a fence

on little un-Grecian Ern's
shoulders and I'd hooted

at Eric's speechless
English leer as he beheld

unseen teams of Swedish nudists
bouncing their balls

20th–22nd August 2020

Written on the Day that Mr Bo was Committed to Prison

Times Radio drones its truth to
power itself. Bo's shut away,

violator of his word, yet in his flattered
state all's a lark. He

hasn't killed 40,000
through grandeur's neglect.

Our despoiler of both domestic
ties and international law

attempts to glue
the 3½ nations back, like his

busted bust of Pericles. He clutches
his Lucretius ('holiday reading!'

he called it at his trial) who
proves all things play mutant algorithmic

tricks, from atoms to plagues for mortal
remains. Nothing to worry about (the

Cum said, in defence). Not even love,
thinks *our* Adonis of Loveliness,

hoisting himself in happy flights of
fantasy with the next future ex-

Mrs Bo! I know this is just a
thought-experiment, the fictional

culling of his wrecking crew,
since the real delusive Bo

is pounding out his podium's latest
legend, *SHIT – SHOWER – SHIRT:*

BRITAIN'S BACK TO WORK, and it's me
who's banged up with a bastard sonnet.

10th September 2020

Keen, fitful gusts are whisp'ring here and there

Faithful guests whisper filth
in this overdub

Understudies in thorny thickets
flushing their pumps

This poem was only picked
for its references to Petrarch

Let's skim the frosty stars
distancing in constellations

The threaded illuminations at
Blackpool clustering my dead poems

Ignore the chesty chill queuing
at the remote testing centre

Contrafacts **testing testing
testing** the spumes of brimful song

I take back control of these
miles to go or we'll soon be

Trotting to Robert Frost's measures
I assume direct rule until I'm

Safe back home with my bust
of Blake frowning under the weight of

Lardy impressions re-musicating
Milton's subaltern devilry

Sublunary Blowup Laura blushes
behind her light green face covering

As fitful Keats crested in laurels
flusters like Bo at PMQs with

His moonshot galaxy-beating
bluster his lust a pump to inflate her

17th September 2020

Great Spirits Now on Earth are Sojourning

Vile men have been among us
Bo brushes tousled straw

Eyes watery weak he who
On Chequers plain drops

In post-viral fatigue then
Forges restrictions as a chain

For freedom's sake And Go!
Who waits for rosy spring when

Dover's gridlock and lockdown
Are down and his social smile will

Morph into an unmasked bite
In a city-centre Pret sandwich

The Age of the Cum will hum
With broken treaties and threats

Whispering the Rule of Sixes or
Sevens as the 1922 Committee

Perches on futurity's frown their
Thinking must purchase wishes

With another will and will tell
Of mighty workings **redaction**

   redaction   **redaction**
Shut up World listen to Bo's

Exceptionalist script Britain
Invented strict freedom and

Sold it to the English as licence which
Is why some won't fit their hooters

Into Chinese masks or leave the
Lock-in chain pub at curfew

23rd September 2020

Good Kosciusko, thy great name alone

Bo, your bright syllable
pops like corn,

sprays us with beneficent
seed, amid

'collective forbearance'. The
'iron laws of geometrical

progression' clatter
under the everlasting Covid-rabid

splutter of your hymn
to 'commonsense'. 'Our'

NHS Heroes are now
small change trilling above

the testing cash-rich crashing
of tills until you tell,

forever stealing
round the British throne,

that on that
happy Brexit day

of no test no track no
trace no deal, yes,

your name with papery
Chamberlain shall be twined!

You're gently mingling,
promising 'tremendous' bits

and 'fantastic' bobs far
far away where the great unmasked Go

patrols for evermore the
cloudless lorry parks of Kent.

1st October 2020

After dark vapours have oppressed our plains

Dark vapours have depressed our plans
throughout these anxious months. I'm fed up!

The blasted spaces of this blighted nation Bo
may patrol but cannot control. *He's* fed up,

Come-A-Day Bo of the gentle South, clearing
the North for sleek railway bridges,

charmed wind farms
churning under the sick heavens.

'I am like the Magic-Laureate of an
Infected Land,' Bo-de-liar declares,

ennuied. He leaves the unseemly stains
of his wizardy wand as he relieves himself

of our long, lost rites. Fed up with the lost
statistics of this second wave, he cries

'I am like infectious Trump
sealed in The Beast, breathing grim

on the bulletproof smoked glass!'
Our eyes with gathering fever blur.

Rosy on a policy drip, I'm fed up with
calming strategies – eating out –

pottering around un-sprouted lettuce
in the yard – the milky

autumn sun behind pearl clouds that
glimmers across the faces of fed up freshers

locked in trauma bubbles with strangers –
lost between the lost lines of Sappho –

fed up with egg timer haiku – but never
with this life mask of Keats above my desk.

(apologies to Nicholas Moore)

6th October 2020

On Seeing the Elgin Marbles

Bo's body and spirit weak
though morality weighs light

on a sleepless night
'negotiating'

lockdown Liverpool's
hardship fund till

morning's dull eye finds
blushing Europe demanding

its sugar-cube moebles
back in exchange for 'our'

free-spawned English fish
Bo's ill-conceived glories

of post-Brexit grandeur
spin in the dizzy feud

between hawkish anti-maskers
and those sick as a parrot

with Dido's indescribable
classic catastrophe though

I could describe a
limping six foot Lord imploring

'English free-born men to spare
what once was free'

although I am forced (by
Eng.Lit plc) to watch

our Onanistic Mankin dripping
over Athena's stumps

reduced to trickling honeyed phrases
into the armpit of the English sonnet

12th October 2020

2. Curtal Song-Nets from Junkets

Keats' Bright Star, would I were as steadfast as thou art *came into Bell's head, but he was quick enough to see that the end of this would be most appallingly and pertinently romantic.*

    'Are you interested in the stars?' *he said, with a new clever idea in his mind.* 'In Astronomy?'

    'Yes', *said Gertrude.* 'I like hearing about Astrology.'

—Patrick Hamilton, *The West Pier*

If by dull rhymes our English must be chained

If rhyme's a crime, it
fetters Bo to Go, leaves

The musty song-net a
dungeon with

Whips and gags (and
Covid-Secure handwash). So

I've taken insoles
from my slippers,

Put in my own, Oulipean
constraints to

Curtail this slipping on
dead leaves. Let's

Inspect the liar and
his new Tier 3

Rules. I leave the house
in my homemade mask for

Contactless commerce with
my boundless Muse. If

Bo may not set
the English free

(they'll tie themselves in nots

22nd October 2020

Fame, like a wayward girl, will still be coy

As we fall
for a footballer with balls,

the unpopular populist
goes *POP!* Wooing

with lunch pack,
kneeling like a euro-slave,

shy Bo licks
the heels of 'scandalous'

Dame Dido, Mistress
Ozymandias from

Carry On Up the Sphinx!
I'll not speak of those

who will not learn to
govern with consent.

Bo's jilted Burnham, his
luscious eyebrows,

his rugged cagoule,
his lockdown logic.

You poets with prizes
'providing'

lovelorn
lunchbox 'content'
if she likes you on
Twitter she'll follow you back

28th October 2020

O thou! whose face hath felt the winter's wind

Hey, red face, out in the
Storm, have you seen

Hail pelting windscreens
Like spore balls? Anti-

Vaxxer, feasting on the dark
Web's fly, free-speeching

*ASK FOR A MASK? RISK
MY FIST!* Christ-

Mas shall be your season,
Shopping and disease.

Don't fret after knowledge: I
Claim negative capability,

Like a Test and Trace
Consultant peddling my ignorance,

Or a Brexpert who thinks
A thought of free trade

Cannot be traded
Free! They're only *arguably*

Asleep who think
Themselves awake

(I wouldn't know[1]

4th November 2020

---

[1] One reads Keats's term 'negative capability' like Olson read it, as the willed suspension of the lyrical ego, and it is that, but the whole passage, in his letter of December 1817, needs to be read circumspectly. It alerts one not just to Coleridge's

oppositional 'positive capability' (as nobody calls it); Keats's supposition of 'a fine isolated verisimilitude caught from the Penetralium of mystery' is surely a *parody* of the turbocharged certainty one finds in Coleridge, man and writer. Abstruse neologistic motormouthism for a simple fact.

Faced with that, I think I would fold my self away like an untouched picnic hamper and assume the protean trans-inhabitable haunting that Keats sees as the essence of Shakespeare's being. Borges is more to the point when he calls this essence of Shakespearean quality 'everything and nothing', the man 'many and no one', the writing multiple *and* singular. Not neutrality, but neutral capability.

'O fret not after knowledge!' doesn't imply turning from knowledge at all. Keats had the kind of medical knowledge we rely upon so much at the moment; he never disparaged that, or his conscious knowledge of the English poets, of whom he wished to be 'among'. He didn't 'have none' of knowledge, as his sonnet's narrator claims (twice), but he did risk 'being in uncertainties'. 'Fretting' for it is neither a passive 'thirst' for knowledge, nor an active 'pursuit' of it: it is an anxiety that paralyses its acquisition, thwarts the efficacy of knowledge gained.

In these times, I think of Bertrand Russell's summary of the ethics in Stefan Themerson's writing: 'The world contains too many people believing too many things, and it may be that the ultimate wisdom is contained in the precept that the less we believe, the less harm we shall do.'

When I Have Fears that I May Cease to Be

When Bo has fears that
Trump may cease to be

President before his
Twittering thumbs have

Scraped the cracker-barrel
Clean shredded Bo's Brexuberant emails

I trace shadows with the magic
Thumbs of *schadenfreude*

While Trump re-counts
Votes until they count against him

Never may Bo look upon himself
As he sees Trump now as a

Cloudy mirror of unreflective
Spite standing alone

On the shores of the World
Wide Web he

Violates Twitter he
Defames women

'Well on his way to
Decompensating'

    (whatever that means

9th November 2020

Why Did I Laugh Tonight? No Voice will Tell

No voice will tell them,
not even in verse. Bo roams

the hellish hollows of
a self-isolate Number 10;

the Cum's shot off through
the letterbox, spraying reporters.

Bo 'resets', upsets
the Scots (and his bottle of

scotch), ignores
Covid-dark

Noël and Brexpeditious
Hogmanay. Trump

squats amid his gaudy signs
in the democratic

haven of 'his' Whitest House,
tapping out caps *I WON!*

Caffeinated, he ignores his Narrative
Consultant, twitters on.

He never laughs. Why
do you think *I* laugh?

The leases of these two lardy
lumps of manliness will

> *cease upon a midnight*
> *with no pain*

17th November 2020

I Cry your Mercy – Pity – Love! – Aye, Love!

He cries – piteous love
encloses his heart –

arrest, blockage, betrayal,
boredom –

Monumental monomaniacal
British despair –

Freedom: unmasked
and 'being seen' in Tesco

he breathes over the
moulded plastic matrices –

the Frozen Child slips national
fish through EU nets –

O! milky breast and its million
clicking pleasure-hits! –

the frame of blight –
the self contained –

motionless emotion's black
hole's black hole –

choosing disgust
and ambition blind

(witness
the pain
of others? I've
got enough for
everyone You
pick up

                    the dropped bookmark
                                        but
            you'll never find *that*
                page again –
                    the one that
                        made sense of
                            it all

20th November 2020

Bright star! would I were steadfast as thou art!

Blighted satirist! steady
as I go, sailing

by the seat of Trump's big boy
pants, Bo's little boy peeps,

guided by the singleness
of Brextinguishable stars,

I must fix the target
to hit it: hit, it leaks,

sullies clean waters round
our post-human shores

in Anthropocenic
obscenity, even tonight

gazing on the new soft fallen masks of
safe vaccine volunteers. Yes, I pump

the bouncy castle of my Muse's
plump amusements,

rocking forever, in bitter-
sweet unrest,

the unfixed differences within
her tender respiration

> *(each exploration*
>   *should be*
> *imploration*
> *we're either going on or*
>   *we're going off*

        on one

24th November 2020

Lift not the painted veil:
an overdub of Shelley

Drop your Union Jack mask! Real things,
not unlike conspiracies, are printed there,
miming, through the make-believe of garment
technology, unbeliefs unthreaded by
'those twin imposters, rigour and imagination'.
The thingness of art unsustains stringiness of substance.

Dropping his mask from his bulky beak,
his wrinkled lips, Booster Bo boasts,
'This vaccine is a shot in the arm, a Union
flag brand on the flanks of herded Brexports!'
The 'urban', unheeding, refuse first divvies.
The threat of a logistic sergeant's pointing blade
spirits bright blots of blood in the gloomy homeland's
shaded groves, untrusted colonial truths.

2nd December 2020

Unth(reading) Clare

The Gipsy Camp

The snow falls deep; the forest lies alone.
The boy goes hasty for his load of brakes,
Then thinks upon the fire and hurries back.
The gipsy knocks his hands and tucks them up,
And seeks his squalid camp, half hid in snow,
Beneath the oak, which breaks away the wind,
And bushes close, with snow like hovel warm.
There stinking mutton roasts upon the coals,
And the half roasted dog squats close and rubs,
Then feels the heat too strong and goes aloof;
He watches well, but none a bit can spare,
And vainly waits the morsel thrown away.
'Tis thus they live, a picture to the place:
A quiet, pilfering, unprotected race.

John Clare

I've loved thee, Swordy Well, and love thee still

Bo's loved every inch of England well,
feeling his way through parishes like a letch.
Now he's ramping up tests and jabs he can risk
his state-subsidised gerontocidal Yuletide rules!
He freights his 'roly poly' panto to Brussels
to haunt Europe with the spectre of Covid dead:
hunting his dying Brexit deal at a summit supper
of disputed fish and undisputed trifles, capering
his fantasies of Little England or Global Britain.
There's no devil in these details, just level
withdrawal: anatomies of national melancholy,
economies of scaling down, ecologies of collapse.
Quiz the power of this small beer to intoxicate –
his proud nation finds little reason to be proud.

10th December 2020

I love to see the old heath's withered brake

In this poem, I force
myself out of doors,

face the heron flapping
across Greenbank lake –

it tips bold wing over
long-legged arrest, alights

amid a squad
of cormorants that shuffles aside

oily wings in silent grudge.
On the fallen ash stump, a

robin poses, without sharp
trill, all life in its eye –

out of the generation that
love-struck Audubon

sketched here, snatched
in a line's quick fling.

Stranger birds, screeching
parakeets, hide

or are hidden, in a
communal flip and rip

atop the old holly
tree; its unhorned leaves,

grown smooth and
unberried, shake –

not a flash of yellow-green
flitting,

just migrant voices under
the poem's hood.

(i.m. Christopher Middleton)

16th December 2020

The rich brown-umber hue the oaks unfold

Pink clouds lift a late dawn
as they thicken across the sky.

Sun comes up to outshine the
Christmas star left on all night.

So far, so good. Beyond words
of power that Bo crafts for TV,

the English strain mutates
where we live and breathe.

Not so good. One way to represent
this 'Covid Christmas and Brexit New

Year': a thousand nose-to-arse trucks
stuck in Kent's tainted woodlands.

The borders are sealed *against* us. (No
more jokes about national dogging sites.

No luscious nymph squeezes an old
chap dry against a tree in this paradise!)

Flat Matt Pancake's manslaughtery
eye unthreads the governing artifice:

the unrepresentable future
is represented by his blank fear,

the scope of his 'It's out of control!'
Bo scratches his wiry bonce, wishes

he was a backbench Fabricant, rich,
outrageous, and mostly fictional.

The year's hard dusk falls beyond
the falling rain: colour drains

from the day's sketch pad
and the mind alone is alone.

22nd December 2020

The south-west wind, how pleasant in the face

The north-west chill frosts bonnets and windscreens
across the newly independent nation-state of Bressex.
Go, on the news, expounds the Bo-Deal changes
('check passport/insurance/roaming charges…').
A sleek blackbird bounces across the frozen mulch
in songless incursion into magpie's pecking ground,
imperious as those quarantined Brits in the Alps,
an escaping herd at the new hard border.

Bressex, free, sniffs its own armpit, the musk
of Empire. Slaves like bees burrowed into beans,
busy with song, the wild music of luxury. O!
rich disorder of enrichment at the FREEPORT:
our wind farms paddle particulate from the nukes,
as the Covid dead moulder under soft molehills.

28th December 2020

De Wint! I would not flatter nor would I

Skill in critique isn't flattery
(though Bo loves to be liked)

yet in rediffusion of
Petrarch I subtitled his subtle

sex scenes with smut and sleaze! I
painted deadly freaks on Surrey's

coats of arms, left Drayton to fashion
his own out of his vegetable features.

Now I wake up inside romantic sonnets.
Yesterday, I found myself within

one of Wordsworth's on the death
penalty, a magistratic drone denying

mercy (that's Petal Patel sorted
for Bressex Poetry Day). Today,

I scramble out, masked, voice muffled,
glasses steaming, to level

pastures to see how Clare's spots
mark me see that shallow bowl

of field in Sefton Park, filling
with fog, floating scattered crows

in half-fading light, ghostly specks
of silent smoky grey, as hope –

while commonsense sees nothing
but an image of social distancing.

Clare wrote to Dr Darling about
inoculation. Will I run out of poems

to twist into pricks before I get mine?
A magpie skates down the freezing slates.

4th January 2021

Black grows the southern sky betokening rain

You know how this ends: the driving rain
drives you home again. A murder of crows
in the rheumy treetops settles. They feel the
change, no unconscious flapping without will.

Before long, your legs will be denim wet. Trump's
storm troopers stormed. The first drop drops.
Everything focuses *from* this: looking and hearing,
shunning and taking (rolling out a vaccine).

Bouncing in the mulch, the blackbird with
golden beak stops to look at *you*, stopped.
He blurts a curt 'chup-chup', hops where his
brown mate's found thorny shelter from the storm.

No room for you. A thousand deaths a day.
Your best wishes are dreams without horizon.

10th January 2021

What a night! The wind howls, hisses and but stops

I love to wander
the vacated Covid streets

as snow falls slow
on the breeze. A single

flake flukes my pocket,
pricks my bare hand. I

lift it out and smile.
What a night! was ever

said in the soft
safety of morning, sun

burning on snow
heaped by glistening tarmac:

escape for Triumph Herald
with spinning tyres

and gasping motor.
Night allegorised so

that even pissing
at frozen bus stops drunk

prefigured the never-
believed in the un- (yet)-

known, as new
sensations flooded

old memories.
In the windows

of parallel streets: peeling
NHS rainbows from last spring,

BLM placards from
unthinkable summer.

16th January 2021

The oddling bush, close sheltered hedge new-plashed

Clare's going to say 'oddling' if he wants to.
This poem's all tits and bums:

the only human here's a peeping tom.
All the action's avian, and its heroes,

the Stakhanovite builders in the hedges,
implementing instinct's one-year-plan. All

this in the sharp delivery of his gossamer
description. The eggs, 10, he says, or 12,

as though counting them with us, their
'dusts of red soft frittered'. Hope's

fore-shining, in the tiniest traces
of the littlest things that nestle

unscheduled, shatters
against news of the Liverpool Variant.

The song thrush from lockdown 1 reappears,
propped and primed along the chimney stack,

peeping stray notes
like a saxophonist teasing the reed,

constructing disconnected phrases
into languid play of intricate

intermittent melody: cool thoughts of
Ahmad Jamal looking at undepressed keys,

or Miles listening over lowered trumpet,
staging their forthcoming forming in waves

of silent anticipation. Knowledge *is* won.
No hungry peasant contracts Covid-19

just to defraud Bo of five hundred quid!
Soon the sonnet will fill with flustery song.

23rd January 2021

Where slanting banks are always with the sun

The pretty winter lights
are left in windows long

after Christmas this year.
Watch the worker home

in blossoming mask perceive
drily his white collar neighbour

home working in the warm.
The woman across the road

wrestles in wind
a shielding bag over her soft

bike seat; it rustles,
killer's plastic over

a victim's last breath,
upside down Tesco logo.

Snow drops in hell,
Narcissus out of a clump

of uncrumped snow: no
slant is ever

in the sunlight for
ever, flashes

in patches,
acts

latched onto lack. Bo
bows his head; then

crows of his bright Bressex
carnival. One

million years
of human life fall to him.

28th January 2021

I found a ball of grass among the hay

Bo fancies a bit of old fashioned rough in the hay,
mouse's ear'ole, but catches an early bird: that
EU jet patrolling its Border with BOT Ulster
to stop vaccine leaking into Unionist rump…

'You wee, cowran, tim'rous beastie, squeaky toy Bo,
with your brattling Bressexistential Threat!' Sturgeon's
voice, grotesque to Bo's Suddron ear, he tries
a joke! 'Who has "difficulty getting food on to the table?"

A drunken Scot!' A crawling brood can't afford
laptops to do Go's homework on frontal adverbials?
Helpfully, Bo's levelling up. He pumps dirty water
up lead pipes! Domination breaks political union.

Bo's privatised nest of commonsense appetites
festers in his lusty sexpool beneath the setting sun.

30th January 2021

I Love to Hear the Evening Crows Go By

He loves to tell us he
loves to hear that

croaking crew, loves
to see murmuration

modelling helicoid invention,
stark above his haystack. He'll

leave his eaves free for
fugitive sparrows.

A pigeon bobs towards
a neighbour's crumbs.

He muses on that pinch
of stranger blue-green rust,

the kingfisher flitting above its
muddy trickle, and

of high geese's V-ing chorus
to lifted horizons. He

loves to tell him-
self that he loves to work

Mary's fit-as-a-fiddle
body, bowing slow, or

plucking swift, melodies. He pecks
a common ditty,

earned from unclosed
sound, into her open ears.

It murmurs through her
shifted form from lap to lip.

She sings *I love to see I
love to see I love to see…*

6th February 2021

I dreaded walking where there was no path

He dreads his daily walk on narrow pavement
closed in by schoolkids clumping and hugging,
turns away wary of every body's invasive breath
on the free road, zigzagging for a plodding solitude
in which his thoughts may conspire: what hope for hope
if he's tracked and traced by Bo's chipped vaccine
that nationalises and privatises him in one quick jab?
The weak light seeps through tainted clouds and
disperses across his wilding thoughts' dispersal.
Once he fancied every stranger who strayed across
his path was Mary. Now, in the aging abnormal,
he just feels for his mask, stops dead to allow passage
of an absentminded beauty rambling into her phone.
Subject appears to be ruminating proximate to target.

12th February 2021

The brakes like young stag's horns come up in spring

Young stags' horns catch on the brambles
in pursuit of Fanny Fusty down near Doxy's Fen.
They fill the *effing* forest with lusty howls of pain.
On far Kentish hillocks there's buttock room enough
for dog walkers *and* doggers (each with plastic bags).
Nature's horny gift is open country. Thus London
is a rumour of Tory rapers and Whig reformers –
though Bo is pulled hairily through a hedge
for a masked white-coat photo-op, pumping
ersatz vaccine and sponging soapy stools. Watch.
I could not bear to see Go's lorry-park ploughs
scrape dogging sites from the earth's blistered thighs.
I lost my mind sheltering it in lockdown furlough;
I'll walk back to Northborough just to get the jab.

18th February 2021

The snow falls deep, the forest lies alone

Deep snow buries forest deeper into
itself. I think of bracken crackling on
the campfire, for I am great Lord Byron,
laureate tinker of the tinkling jingle!
This gypsy claps his gloves and promises
escape: he leaves me his old hat for luck.
Hastening for hope but hoping for haste,
I feel the heat at my temples singeing
my hair; they've invented electricity
to fry my wits. By wind-break oak the dog
breaks wind, prowls and scowls around the fire.
Mutton drips and hisses. Protected race?
Plague pits re-open; the madhouse locks down.
Bill Gates pilfers profit from my *Don Juan!*

25th February 2021

Astral Zen Knickers
overdub of Shelley's 'To Wordsworth'

Sheppàrd the chanteur wet with lyrical rain
dripping tremulous lines of things that depart
you once sang White Van Man's 'Sweet Thing'
driving the chariot of a dynamite love over
indifferent drinkers in the Shakespeare's Head.
Tell that ancient blues shouter he should shelter.
Better, he should *shut it!* One loss is yours:
you'll never never never sing *that* song again.

Chanteur Shelley cancelled Wordsworth but
not his *songs – still* consecrate to truth and liberty.
'Dick Turpin wore a mask!' So did the gerontologist
who pulled out the brains of survivin' Sir Ivan,
injected them with monkey glands and stuffed
them back in with a pair of Union Jack pants.

27th February 2021

Partly from Hartley

When we were idlers with the loitering rills,
The need of human love we little noted:
Our love was nature; and the peace that floated
On the white mist, and dwelt upon the hills,
To sweet accord subdued our wayward wills:
One soul was ours, one mind, one heart devoted,
That, wisely doting, ask'd not why it doted,
And ours the unknown joy, which knowing kills.
But now I find, how dear thou were to me;
That man is more than half of nature's treasure,
Of that fair Beauty which no eye can see,
Of that sweet music which no ear can measure;
And now the streams may sing for others' pleasure,
The hills sleep on in their eternity.

   Hartley Coleridge

Partly from Hartley: two double sonnets

> *Politically speaking, I am much more a Tory than a Whig, and least of all, a Democrat.*
> Hartley Coleridge

1

*Pops! barred from both houses, from Parliament
for ranting, and from Mop's cottage for raving,
to you I owe the little art of numbers,
'the compound interest of self-interest'
that you taught, even as, peeping over weeping Mop's
shoulder, at me, cradled in my misfortune,
you cursed my constitutional wrongs, asserting
'the natural right of the Right to be right'.
Your curse was enacted: in made up countries
like Portfomandra, by my tyrant imagination,
Lakeland peaks loomed into shapeless judges;
my only exit strategy was to re-write the laws!
If there's any good left in these damaged goods,
I'll dump them on your city mews and scuttle off.*

*It's natural to covet wars that one's missed,
taking pot-shots from the foothills of Empire.
We're willing agents by the gushing spout,
lusting for a greater than individual love,
two little boys with radio-controlled war toys, two
souls, two minds, rivalling into man and master,
master and slave!* I can't do this anymore:
I scripted myself from Burke to Kwarteng,
lockdown reading that locked me down and out!
Caricature keeps bursting from bad character;
translation risks making Bo intelligible! Flatpack
Wordsworthianisms unfolded on Helvellyn
obscure the flares that scare EU Armadas.
Bo's Cyber Force sleeps with one eye open.

2

In my abandoned sonnet, the *two friends*
meet again at a place they loathe, the *pie-*
factory at Leeds, watch people they despise,
hobbling over cobbles, spitting gobs of post-
industrial effluent from once-toiling lungs!
Too busy: one, a businessman with a
smelting coalmine to sink, while our hero's
still buzzy with parental apologia,
that he'd long resolved to ventriloquize.
O! say not so that *he* could play the poem's
part, or to claim that Petrarch's patient love
'parades while sterner duty stamps and stomps'.
To hope without hope, like this, you'd think
he was an Utopian or a fool!

Despair was a bigger deal then, I suppose.
It didn't just mean running out of sonnets
before he'd finished funnelling neurodiversity
into their handy hip-flasks, or discovering Bo's
vaccine pub-pass uses an app he'll never procure;
he'll leave no data trail of his nocturnal rambles!
He calls his girl's soul 'lovely', stainless
Sheffield shine; she'll never reach his love
because he's so pure, he says (but he's no
better than his dad and his crack whores).
His filthy sonnet thinks about her '*every* part',
drips over her kissy-wissy Daguerreotype.
Only then it speaks to him, in the lost voice
of Laura: 'Why ever thus thy days consume?'

March–Easter 2021

To Laughter
an overdub of Shelley

The friends of humour nudge the fiend of wit.
We hoot at Go shaking his lallies on the dancefloor,
hand wheels, flightless wings (almost rainbow vests);
Bo asking the 'guys' who's had emails, 'like him',
pleading futile refuge in Bressex; our Choice Architect
of prisons for protesters and trespassers and children
crouching (with clipboard) over Afghan escapees –
like chickens for Nandos, from Kabul, we depart.
Mockers on it, you can't escape Covid death stats;
but Go bounced icky into the Aberdeen night air,
Bo endorsing Graab's 'the sea was closed' caper,
split the sides of something more than a sonnet.
Not everything true is funny. Laughter *is* slaughter:
One 'sewage-side' bomber did for Global Britain.

30th August 2021

After Laughter

Afterword

The shepherd's brow, fronting forked lightning,
    a late impression from Gerard Manley Hopkins

This poet's brow flashes
forked fire, borrows

catastrophe and chaos
from you know (by now)

who. Tories topple into
second jobs, third

jabs, topping up; or
'watering up' their fluid pledges

to the people, as bags
of unvaxxed bones in the ICU

leak, then leap in last gasp's grip,
where each breath should be our

memento mori. Hand to mouth
on twenty quid a week

less, 'more retail policy offers',
they await 'big picture stuff'.

Bo the man is, just
about, PM, unmasked,

groaning as he dumps
in the NHS privy voiding

with no paper his hangover gush,
avoiding his crawlbaby CBI porkypie babble.

They do not suffer his paper shuffling suffering,
dyspraxic disgrace, his antic tone.

He who undied for us, sudden, espies
his own unfeeling piggy eyes, a mirror flash

along a smooth knife's nice length –
but in *whose* fevered, fiery hand?

25th November 2021

After Image
Improvisation upon Idealism *by Arthur Symons*

We now know that Bo has no
conscience (we always knew),

sad dog-eyes lowered over his mask
(at last) as he 'apologises' to Queen

(and country) for *not* breaking rules,
police at his door, redactions behind. He

was the master of our viral flesh
and of secret lockdown fleshpots.

His wit we admired, faultless
music without fact. 'Not a details

man,' we used to say, as, pissed, he
sprinkled state papers around the flat.

We now know he cannot tell the truth:
of kitsch wallpaper, crime statistics,

Brexit and Covid (his twins!),
children (more twins?) and parties,

ambushing labour with divinest wine
from his fridge, thirsting afresh! As we

vainly implore his overthrow, Bo
throws the party opposite over

with memes of Jimmy Savile (in truth, *his*
twin, blonde residue on our perfect body).

Tyrannous, he craves the power
he once had (over us), his mind

a mumble of deceit, the grumbling party
a tight-lipped instrument that he

can no longer finger
to scratch his extempore ditties.

9th February 2022

Aftershock

*Monitoring Adam Mickiewicz' first
Crimean Sonnet: The Ackerman Steppe*

Who sails the arid Ocean
of the steppes in his Skoda,

ploughing through, plunging
into, green expanse, the wheat-waves?

Whatever flower of the
flood grows now is picked for its rhyme

in these variant
translations, for I am not *there*.

No light. No road. No stars.
He searches the skies for a guide,

but it pours fire in his eyes
from the East (all translation

is stunned into cliché). Is this
the end of curfew? the dawn?

the ancient lighthouse
of Bilhorod-Dnistrovskyi burning,

or the city, burning? *They* are near.
Stop! Listen! He hears cranes or goats

flinching under hawks or falcons. I
translate them into Ukrainians and

Russians, Molotovs and missiles,
militia wriggling in the mud and

snaking tank columns stuck on the road. In
the hush he listens for voices from the West,

but there is only the hush. Bo boasts
our refuge record, the sanctions we sanction;

he's still thinking of those party bottles
that will never be filled with petrol.

3rd March 2022

After Sheppàrd After Shelley: England in 2022

Bo, despised now but boosterish, resigns –
finishes off himself and the Queen with a bow!

Through public scorn of this politician, springs
muddled Truss, without knowledge or feeling,

syphoning our last reserves. The Queen drops,
into 'our' 'cost of living crisis', 'dead'

to quote the caption of the little girl's sketch
that proud Dad magnetized to the empty fridge.

Mannequins in mourning peer facelessly
from over-lit sex shop windows, Brexit

borders sealed for one silent minute, while
Time stands stagnant, our escape route

blocked by bridges raised 'in honour',
cranes lowered 'with respect'. Subjects

respond with cargo cult carvings:
Thames mud sculptures, bat-faced

effigies propped up on cartoon limbs
beside closed public loos, shut hospitals.

Flowers are sprinkled on Holocaust
memorials and designated dumps.

Police club a lost rollerblader
to the ground, while crowds cheer

the regal recycling van (oh! tempestuous
mourning bursts along the Covid Wall).

I hold up a blank sheet of paper to protest
against elegies by Duffy and Armitage.

Once the lad is lifted to his rollerskated feet,
he's wheeled off to the police van – and so am I!

19th September 2022

Notes and Acknowledgements

British Standards is the third book of a trilogy, 'The English Strain', the previous parts consisting of *The English Strain*, Bristol: Shearsman Books, 2021, and *Bad Idea*, Newton-le-Willows: Knives Forks and Spoons Press, 2021.

Notes to '14 Standards'

The title refers to the practices and procedures of Anthony Braxton's 'Standards' ensembles (see Braxton 2004). All the 'standards' selected for these cover versions are found in Feldman and Robinson 1999. They are, with their full titles:

1 William Lisle Bowles, 'To the River Tweed'
2 Samuel Taylor Coleridge, 'To a Friend, Who Asked How I Felt, When the Nurse First Presented My Infant to Me'
3 John Thelwall, 'The Vanity of National Grandeur'
4 Robert Southey, 'Poem on the Slave Trade (III)'
5 Anna Seward, 'To a Young Lady, Purposing to Marry a Man of Immoral Character in the Hope of his Reformation'
6 Mary F. Johnson, 'The Idiot Girl'
7 Mary Tighe, 'Written at Killarney. July 29, 1800'
8 Leigh Hunt, 'The Nile'
9 Horace Smith, 'Ozymandias'
10 Thomas Hood, 'Written in the Workhouse'
11 Charles Tennyson Turner, 'When lovers' lips from kissing disunite'
12 Hartley Coleridge, 'Long time a child, and still a child'
13 Letitia Elizabeth Landon, 'The Dancing Girl'
14 Dante Gabriel Rossetti from 'Sonnets for Pictures: A Dance of Nymphs, Andrea Mantegna; in the Louvre'

Standard 1. Byron called Bowles 'the maudlin prince of mournful sonneteers', a crown I covet. (Hunt 1990: 194)

Standard 9. Horace Smith's sonnet was written at the same time as Shelley's 'Ozymandias'. (See my 'dub' of the latter in the present volume.) Both sonnets were published in Hunt's *Examiner* during 1818. Guy Davenport points out that the poem, which appears as 'Ozymandias' in Feldman and Robinson, was originally entitled 'On a Stupendous Leg of Granite, Discovered Standing by Itself in the Deserts of Egypt, with the Inscription Inserted Below', and comments, 'Shelley called his "Ozymandias". Genius may also be knowing how to title a poem.' (Davenport 1984: 281) This remark may be extended to several of the originals of these Standards. However, Smith's spectacle of the 'annihilated' London of futurity is a memorable vision not shared by Shelley's poem (Davenport shows how much Shelley took from Smith). This partly explains my choice of this 'Ozymandias', but my poem 'for Stephen', written in 2007, is already a transposition of Shelley's justly more famous sonnet, and I would like to interject it here, for contrast with my versions of Smith and Shelley:

> The red metronome on Letná hill
> sways like a lucky drunkard
> on its pedestal above the spires
> a restless reminder of rust and wreck.
> Or an antique windscreen wiper
>
> describing its arc
> upon a plane of smear and rain-wash
> heroic in a monochrome movie, tinted red
>
> With each wipe across the screen
> the determined visage of the driver clears.
> It's Josef Stalin the giant blocks with his pocks
> long blown to shatters but he's still there
>
> waving yes and no
> to anyone who can see him (Sheppard 2007: 112)

Note to 'Tabitha and Thunderer'

Sappho and Phaon by Mary Robinson was published in 1796. 'Tabitha and Thunderer': Tabitha Bramble (a lift from Smollett) was one of Robinson's pen names, the 'English Sappho' another, to add to her many disreputable nicknames, such as 'Perdita', after the role she played on stage (with her lover, Prince George, becoming 'Florizel' in the celebrity media of the times). 'The Thunderer' was a print by James Gillray that features

Robinson (impaled on a whirligig pole) and her lover, Banastre Tarleton, the Liverpudlian gambler, warrior and Member of Parliament (or debtor, war criminal and slave owner). His family have streets named after it in Liverpool, a sudden live issue with the Black Lives Matter movement of Summer 2020, when I was writing the poem, and the country was coming out of the first Coronavirus lockdown. The best place for a detailed life of Robinson is Byrne 2005. Tarleton is featured in Cameron and Crooke 1992. Both were glamorous fashion-icons. Mary was an abolitionist at the year she died (1800), by which time she had stopped moving in louche company, becoming first a Foxian Whig (and lover of Charles Fox) and eventually mixing in radical and literary circles, knowing William Godwin and Coleridge, for example; she wrote a poem in praise of the latter's 'Kubla Khan' before he published it, as alluded to here, as are some of her own other poems and elements of biography. All 44 sonnets of *Sappho and Phaon* (and its equally extraordinary feminist introduction) may be found in Feldman and Robinson 1999. It was the first narrative sonnet sequence since the Renaissance. It tells of a heterosexual relationship in Sappho's life, one that led to her anguished suicide. I couldn't let my poem follow the plot of the original (which can be traced through the sequence of expressive titles listed below).

My poem uses the following sonnets in this order:

IV	Sappho Discovers Her Passion
VIII	Her Passion Increases
IX	Laments the Volatility of Phaon
XIII	She Endeavours to Fascinate Him
XV	Phaon Awakes
XVIII	To Phaon
XIX	Suspects His Constancy
XXIII	Sappho's Conjectures (with XXII Phaon Forsakes Her)
XXV	To Phaon
XXX	Bids Farewell to Lesbos
XXXII	Dreams of a Rival
XXXVI	Her Confirmed Despair
XXXIX	To the Muses
XLIII	Her Reflections on the Leucadian Rock Before She Perishes

My own edited selection of Robinson's work, including 'Sappho and Phaon', is published as a Shearsman Classic (2024).

Note to 'Partly from Hartley'

These double sonnets refer to the following poems by Hartley Coleridge, found in all three editions listed, though I worked from Coleridge 1908: 'Dedicatory Sonnet', p. 2; 'When we were idlers with the loitering rills', p. 3; 'In the great city we are met again', p. 3; 'I loved thee once, when every thought of mine,' p. 5. Allusions to, memories of, the following poems also manifest: 'We parted on the mountains, as two streams', p. 4; 'I left the land where men with Nature dwelling', p. 15; ''Tis strange to me, who long have seen no face', p. 15; and to 'From Petrarch', p. 93.

Acknowledgements

Poems from this volume have previously appeared in the following journals: *A) Glimpse) Of)*, *Anthropocene*, *Beir Bua*, *Blackbox Manifold*, *International Times*, *Litter*, *Overground Underground*, *Parmenar Press*, *Pages*, *Peter Barlow's Cigarette Sample Pack 42*, *The Café Review*, *Talking About Strawberries All of the Time*, *Tears in the Fence*, *Shearsman*, *Stride*, and on the *New Boots and Pantisocracies* and *Poetry and Covid* websites, and commissioned as part of the WOW Festival 2020 online anthology, 'Lockdown Unlocked'. I would like to thank all the enterprising editors and curators for their work.

Resources

Anon. ed. *The Poetry of The Anti-Jacobin*. London: Longman, Rees, Orme, Brown and Green, John Hatchard and Son, John Murray, and James Duncan, 1828.
Bate, Jonathan. *John Clare: A Biography*. London: Picador, 2004.
Bate, Jonathan. *Radical Wordsworth: The Poet who Changed the World*. London: William Collins, 2020.
Birkan-Berz, Carole, Guillaume Coatalen and Thomas Vuong, eds. *Translating Petrarch's Poetry: L'Aura del Petrarca from the Quattrocento to the 21st Century*. Oxford: Legenda, 2020.
Borges, J.L. *Labyrinths*. Harmondsworth: Penguin, 1970.
Braxton, Anthony. *23 Standards (Quartet) 2003*, Leo Records, CD LR 402/405 (CD), 2004.
Burgess, Anthony. *ABBA ABBA*. London: Faber and Faber, 1977.
Bussey-Chamberlain. Prudence. *Coteries*. Newton-le-Willows: Knives Forks and Spoons, 2018.

Byrne, Paula. *Perdita: The Life of Mary Robinson*. London: Harper Perennial, 2005.

Byron, *The Works of Lord Byron*. Ware: Wordsworth Editions Ltd., 1994.

Cameron, Gail, and Stan Crooke, *Liverpool – Capital of the Slave Trade*. Liverpool: Picton Press, 1992.

Clare, John. ed. Jonathan Bate. *Selected Poems*. London: Faber and Faber, 2004.

Clare, John. eds. Eric Robinson and David Powell. *The Major Works*. Oxford and New York: Oxford World Classics, 2004.

Coleridge, Hartley. *Poems, Songs and Sonnets* (Leeds: F. E. Bingley, 1833); online version: archive.org/details/poemssongssonnet00cole/page/n4/mode/2up (accessed 11th March 2021)

Coleridge, Hartley. *Poems*. London: Moxon, 1851, ed. with a memoir by his brother Derwent; online at archive.org/details/poemscolerid1coleuoft/page/clxviii/mode/2up (accessed 11th March 2021)

Coleridge, Hartley. *The Complete Poetical Works of Hartley Coleridge*. ed. Ramsay Colles, London and New York: George Routledge and Co., 1908.

Coleridge, Hartley. *Letters of Hartley Coleridge*. ed. Griggs, E.G. and E.L. Griggs. London: Oxford University Press, Humphrey Milford, 1936.

Coleridge, Samuel Taylor. 'Kubla Khan' in Coleridge, ed. H.J. Jackson. *The Major Works*. Oxford, New York: Oxford University Press, 1985.

Coleridge, Samuel Taylor. ed. H.J. Jackson. *The Major Works*. Oxford, New York: Oxford University Press, 1985.

Cummings, Dominic. *Blog* at dominiccummings.com. (accessed 4th May 2021).

Daunt, Will. *Gerard Manley Hopkins: The Lydiate Connections*. Ormskirk: Ormskirk Imprint, 2019.

Davenport, Guy. *The Geography of the Imagination*. London: Picador, 1984.

Feldman, Paula, R., and Daniel Robinson. eds. *A Century of Sonnets*. Oxford, New York: Oxford University Press, 1999.

Davis, Amanda Blake, '"Ephemeral are Gay Gulps of Laughter": P. B. Shelley, Louis MacNeice, and the Ambivalence of Laughter', *English*, vol. 70, no. 268, Spring 2021, 23-46.

Gigante, Denise. *The Keats Brothers*. Cambridge, London: Harvard University Press, 2011.

Gill, Stephen, ed. *The Cambridge Companion to Wordsworth*. Cambridge: Cambridge University Press, 2003.

Gittings, Robert. *John Keats*. Harmondsworth: Penguin, 1971.

Gittings, Robert. ed. *Letters of John Keats*. Oxford and New York: Oxford University Press, 1970.

Godfrey, Richard and Mark Hallett. *James Gillray: The Art of Caricature*. London: Tate Publishing, 2001.

Guattari, Felix. *The Three Ecologies*. London, New Brunswick: The Athlone Press, 2000.

Hamilton, Patrick. *The West Pier*. London: Readers Union/Constable, 1953.

Hazlitt, William, 'On Mr Wordsworth's Excursion', in ed. Gregory Dart.

Metropolitan Writings. Manchester: Carcanet, 2005.
Hazlitt, William. *The Spirit of the Age and The English Poets.* London and Toronto: Dent and Sons, 1910.
Healey, Nicola. *Dorothy Wordsworth and Hartley Coleridge; The Poetics of Relationship.* PhD thesis, University of St Andrews, 2008, at research-repository.st- andrews.ac.uk/bitstream/handle/10023/787/NicolaHealeyPhDThesis.pdf?sequence=6 (accessed 11th March 2021).
Holmes, Richard. *Coleridge: Darker Reflections.* London: Flamingo, 1999.
Hopkins, Gerard Manley, ed. WH Gardner, *Gerard Manley Hopkins.* Harmondsworth: Penguin Books, 1953.
Hopkins, Gerard Manley, eds. WH Gardner and NH MacKenzie. *The Poems of Gerard Manley Hopkins.* Oxford: Oxford Paperbacks, 1970.
Hunt, Leigh. ed. David Jesson Dibley. *Selected Writings.* Manchester: Carcanet, 1990.
Keats, John. ed. H.W. Garrod. *Poetical Works.* Oxford and New York: Oxford University Press, 1970.
Kötting, Andrew. *By Our Selves.* (film), Vimeo.
Kövesi, Simon, *John Clare: Nature, Criticism and History.* Palgrave Macmillan: London, 2017.
Kövesi, Simon, and Erin Lafford, eds. *Palgrave Advances in John Clare Studies.* Palgrave Macmillan: Cham, 2020.
Leader, Zachary. *Revision and Romantic Authorship.* Oxford, New York: Oxford University Press, 1996.
Lucretius, *On the Nature of the Universe,* trans. Ronald Melville. Oxford, New York: Oxford World Classics, 1999.
Maturin, Charles Robert. ed. Victor Sage. *Melmoth the Wanderer.* London: Penguin Books, 2000.
Mickiewicz, Adam, trans. Edna Worthley Underwood, The Crimean Sonnets, 1917, at www.gutenberg.org/files/27069/27069-h/27069-h.htm.
Middleton, Christopher. *Carminalenia.* Manchester: Carcanet, 1980.
Middleton, Christopher. 'Eight Skips around the Aura of Erato', *Two Horse Wagon Going By.* Manchester: Carcanet, 1986.
Moore, Nicholas, *Spleen.* London: Menard Press, 1990.
Pootam, Karim. 'Poetry in Translation – The Akerman Steppe' at karimpootam.wordpress.com/2015/04/29/hello-world/, 2015.
Raghavan, Harish. *Calls for Action.* Whirlwind Recordings, WR4749 (CD), 2019.
Ricks, Christopher. *Keats and Embarrassment.* London, Oxford, New York: Oxford University Press, 1974.
Robinson, Jeffrey C. *Untam'd Wing: Riffs on Romantic Poetry.* Barrytown: Station Hill of Barrytown, 2010.
Robinson, Jeffrey C. '"STC" (By Two Female Poets)', in Jeffrey C. Robinson, *Romantic Presences: Living Images from the Age of Wordsworth and Shelley.* New York: Station Hill, 1995.

Robinson, Mary. *The Poetical Works of the Late Mrs. Mary Robinson, Volume 2.* London: Richard Phillips, 1806; *Scholar Select* facsimile reprint; np: nd.

Robson, Andy. 'Mary Halvorson's Code Girl: *Artlessly Falling*', *Jazzwise* 258, December 2020/January 2021: 40.

Roe, Nicholas, *Fiery Heart: The First Life of Leigh Hunt.* London: Pimlico, 2005.

Russell, Bertrand, 'Preface' to Stefan Themerson, *Professor Mmaa's Lecture.* Woodstock, NY: The Overlook Press, 1984.

Shelley, P.B. *Poetical Works.* London and New York, Frederick Warne and Co., n.d.

Shelley, P.B. *Shelley's Poetry and Prose*, eds. Donald H. Reiman and Sharon B. Powers. New York and London: W.W. Norton, 1977.

Sheppard, Robert. *Warrant Error.* Exeter: Shearsman Books, 2007.

Sheppard, Robert. 'Ode to a Nightingale', in *The Only Life*. Newton-le-Willows: Knives Forks and Spoons, 2011.

Sheppard, Robert. 'Poetics in Anticipation: Shifting an Imaginary', *New Defences of Poetry*, ed. David O'Hanlon-Alexandra, Newcastle Centre for the Literary Arts, University of Newcastle, at nclacommunity.org/newdefences/2021/07/16/shifting-an-imaginary-poetics-in-anticipation, 2021.

Sinclair, Iain. *Edge of Orison.* London: Hamish Hamilton, 2005.

Springs, Kandace. *The Women Who Raised Me.* Blue Note Records, LC 00148 (CD), 2020.

Thornton RKR, and Marion Thane, eds., *Poetry of the 1890s.* London: Penguin, 1997.

Trump, Mary. 'On the Dean Obeidallah Show', November 5th 2020, youtube.com/watch?v=xJ_el9ykdgg&feature=emb_title (accessed 9th November 2020).

Wallen, Byron. *Portrait.* Twilight Jaguar, TJCD3 (CD), 2020.

Westbrook, Mike. *Glad Day: Settings of William Blake.* Enja Records, ENJ-9376 3 (CD), 1999.

Wolfson, Susan J. *Formal Charges: The Shaping of Poetry in British Romanticism.* Stanford: Stanford University Press, 1997.

Wolfson, Susan J. ed. *The Cambridge Companion to Keats.* New York: Cambridge University Press, 2001.

Wordsworth, William. ed. Thomas Hutchinson and Ernest de Selincourt. *Poetical Works.* London, Oxford, New York: Oxford University Press, 1969.

Wordsworth, William. ed. J.C. Maxwell. *The Prelude: A Parallel Text.* Harmondsworth, Penguin, 1971.

Wu, Duncan, ed. *Romanticism: an anthology.* Third edition. Malden and Oxford: Blackwell Publishing, 2007.

Wu, Duncan. *Hazlitt: The First Modern Man.* Oxford and New York: Oxford University Press, 2008.

Zipes, Jack. *Ernst Bloch: The Pugnacious Philosopher of Hope.* Cham: Palgrave Macmillan, 2019.

Zuccato, Edoardo. *Petrarch in Romantic England.* Basingstoke: Palgrave Macmillan, 2008.

www.ingramcontent.com/pod-product-compliance
Lightning Source LLC
Chambersburg PA
CBHW031635160426
43196CB00006B/423